NATURE! WILD AND WONDERFUL

by

Laurence Pringle

photographs by

Tim Holmstrom

Richard C. Owen Publishers, Inc.
Katonah, New York

Richard C. Owen Publishers, Inc.
PO Box 585
Katonah, New York 10536

Library of Congress Cataloging-in-Publication Data

Pringle, Laurence P.
            Nature! wild and wonderful / by Laurence Pringle ; photographs by Tim Holmstrom.
            p.   cm. — (Meet the author)
            Summary: A prominent children's book author shares his life, his daily activities, and his creative process, showing how all are intertwined.
            ISBN: 978-1-57274-071-6 (hardcover)
            1. Pringle, Laurence P. — Juvenile literature. 2. Natural history—
Authorship — Juvenile literature. 3. Science writers—Biography—
Juvenile literature. 4. Children's literature— Authorship— Juvenile literature.
[1. Pringle, Laurence P. 2. Authors, American. 3. Authorship.]
I. Holmstrom, Tim, ill. II. Title. III. Series: Meet the author (Katonah, N.Y.)
QH14.P75 1997
808' .066508—dc21   96-53268

Editorial, Art, and Production Director   *Janice Boland*
Production Assistant   *Donna Parsons*
Color separations by Leo P. Callahan Inc., Binghamton, NY

Printed in the United States of America

9 8 7 6 5

To my children, who inspire me with their sense of wonder and curiosity about the world

From the room where I write,
I see wildflowers and trees.
I hear crows and songbirds.
In the spring I hear the peeping of little frogs.

Outdoors, I watch bumblebees visit flowers.
I eat black raspberries.
All these sights, sounds, and tastes remind me
of my boyhood home, a farm in western New York.
They remind me of the place where my curiosity
about nature began.

My father worked in a factory that made cameras and film.
But on weekends he was a farmer.
My brother Gary and I helped take care
of cows, goats, chickens, and a big vegetable garden.

Each day Gary and I walked to a one-room school.
Our teacher taught grades one through eight
in one classroom.
That may seem very crowded,
but there were never more than
twenty students in our school.
My class was the biggest.
I had three classmates!

Sometimes my brother and I didn't get along very well.
And my sisters were too young to be playmates.
But I was never bored. I read many books.
I spent a lot of time roaming woods and fields.
I explored ponds and springs.
I was curious about nature
and felt close to all living things.

When I was fifteen I began to keep a nature journal.

Bob-white

Killdeer

CAT Bird

In it I wrote of birds seen, nests found,
and of animals tracked in the snow.
I made drawings of favorite birds.
I took photographs and dreamed of being
a wildlife photographer.
In college I studied wildlife biology.
I thought I would study wild animals all my life.
And in a way, I have.

When I was in college I began to write articles
for nature and outdoor magazines.
Then for seven years I was an editor of
Nature and Science, a children's magazine.

nature and science

VOL. 3 NO. 18 / JULY 25, 1966

The
AMAZING
WORLD of
WATER

CREDITS: Pp. 3, 10, 12, photos by Franklyn K. Lauden; pp. 3-7, 10-13, 15, 16, drawings by Graphic Arts Department, The American Museum of Natural History; p. 6, photo courtesy United States Department of Agriculture; p. 8, photos, top by Phil Palmer from FPG, middle by Christopher Schuberth, bottom courtesy the National Park Service; p. 9, photos, top by Herbert Lanks from FPG, bottom by Bradford Washburn; p. 13, photo by N. E. Beck, Jr. from National Audubon Society; p. 14, left photo by George Cope from Educational Services Incorporated, right and p. 15, photos by Verne N. Rockcastle.

PUBLISHED FOR
THE AMERICAN MUSEUM OF NATURAL HISTORY
BY THE NATURAL HISTORY PRESS
A DIVISION OF DOUBLEDAY & COMPANY, INC.

MANAGING EDITOR Franklyn K. Lauden; SENIOR EDITOR Laurence P. Pringle; ASSOCIATE EDITOR Marianne Polachek; EDITORIAL ASSISTANT Linda Britton; ART DIRECTOR Joseph M. Sedacca; ASSOCIATE ART DIRECTOR Donald B. Clausen

CONSULTING EDITORS Roy A. Gallant; James K. Page, Jr.

PUBLISHER Richard K. Winslow; CIRCULATION DIRECTOR J. D. Broderick; SUBSCRIPTION SERVICE Alfred Thiem

NATIONAL BOARD OF EDITORS
PAUL F. BRANDWEIN, CHAIRMAN, Assistant to President, Harcourt Brace & World, Inc.; Dir., Pinchot Institute for Conservation Studies. J. MYRON ATKIN, Co-Dir., Elementary-School Science Project, University of Illinois. THOMAS G. AYLESWORTH, Editor, Books for Young Readers, Doubleday & Company, Inc. DONALD BARR, Headmaster, The Dalton Schools, New York City. RAYMOND E. BARRETT, Dir. of Education, Oregon Museum of Science and Industry. MARY M. BLATT, Science Specialist, Pennsylvania Dept. of Public Instruction. WILLIAM L. DEERING, Science Education Consultant, Huntington, N.Y. ELIZABETH HONE, Professor of Education, San Fernando State College, Calif. GERARD PIEL, Publisher, Scientific American. SAMUEL SCHENBERG, Dir. of Science, Board of Education, New York City. DAVID WEBSTER, Staff Teacher, The Elementary School Science Project of Educational Services Incorporated. • REPRESENTING THE AMERICAN MUSEUM OF NATURAL HISTORY: FRANKLYN M. BRANLEY, Astronomer, The American Museum-Hayden Planetarium; JOSEPH M. CHAMBERLAIN, Asst. Director, AMNH; SUNE ENGELBREKTSON, Chmn. Dept. of Education; GORDON R. REEKIE, Chmn. Dept. of Exhibition and Graphic Arts; DONN E. ROSEN, Chmn. Dept. of Ichthyology; HARRY L. SHAPIRO, Curator of Physical Anthropology.

NATURE AND SCIENCE is published for The American Museum of Natural History by The Natural History Press, a division of Doubleday & Company, Inc., fortnightly, October through April; monthly, September, May, June and July (June and July special issues). Second Class postage paid at Garden City, N.Y. and at additional office. Copyright © 1966 The American Museum of Natural History. All Rights Reserved. Printed in U.S.A. Editorial Office: The American Museum of Natural History, Central Park West at 79th Street, New York, New York 10024.

SUBSCRIPTION PRICES in U.S.A. and Canada: 85 cents per semester per pupil, $1.50 per school year (16 issues) in quantities of 10 or more subscriptions to the same address. Teacher's Edition with single subscription to student's edition $4.50 per school year. Single copy 20 cents. Single subscription per calendar year (18 issues) $3.25, two years $6. ADDRESS SUBSCRIPTION correspondence to: NATURE AND SCIENCE, The Natural History Press, Garden City, N.Y. Send notice of undelivered copies on Form 3579 to: NATURE AND SCIENCE, The Natural History Press, Garden City, New York 11531.

2

All the articles in this issue of *Nature and Science* are about water. Why write a whole issue about something so common? Even though it is common, water is a very unusual material, as you will find when you read the article beginning on this page. Other articles in the issue suggest dozens of things you can do with water this summer, no matter where you happen to be—even on the desert.

■ The earth, unlike any other planet in the solar system, is nearly covered by water. If you could view the earth from space you would see that we live on huge continental islands rising out of a world-wide ocean. None of the other eight known planets in the solar system, in fact, is known to have bodies of liquid water on its surface.

Water is everywhere around you—in the air you breathe, in the ground, even in the desert sand (*see page 6*). It is locked up as ice, it flows through rock pores deep underground, and it makes up most of your body. Even though water is all about us on the earth, surprisingly enough it is one of the most unusual substances in nature.

What makes water "unusual"? For one thing, it can creep uphill against gravity. For another, it is *commonly* found as a liquid, as a solid, and as a gas. During a spring thaw in the north, for example, you often find puddles (liquid water) on the ice (solid water), and water vapor (a gas) in the air above the ice. Or within a single cloud on a summer day, there may be water droplets, water vapor, and ice crystals—all existing at about the same temperature.

Water does not necessarily freeze when the temperature is 32°F. If smoke particles or other pollution wastes are

NATURE AND SCIENCE

A friend encouraged me to try writing a book.
I chose the subject of dinosaurs.
The research was fun.
I have a lively curiosity.
Reading about the facts
and mysteries of dinosaurs was exciting.

But writing was a struggle.

I wrote at night, after work, and after helping my wife Judy take care of our three children: Heidi, Jeffrey, and Sean.

Writing, for me, is often hard work.
Sometimes I try too hard to make a sentence
perfect the first time, instead of writing
a "not so perfect" sentence and making it better later.

My manuscript about dinosaurs was rejected
by eight publishers. Still, I had confidence
in my writing, so I kept trying. Finally, after
almost two years of rejection, my book
Dinosaurs and Their World was published.
My thirtieth book was also about dinosaurs,
as was my seventieth book, *Dinosaurs! Strange and Wonderful.*
Yet each of these books is different from the others.

Every year new dinosaur fossils are discovered
and our understanding of dinosaurs
keeps growing and changing.
Through the years I did some growing and changing, too.

About the time my first book was published
my marriage to Judy ended.
The magazine *Nature and Science* stopped publication.
Since then I have been a freelance writer,
which means I work on my own. I am my own boss.

My curiosity about nature has led me to write about
minnows, vampire bats, coyotes, coral reefs, forest fires,
and killer bees. I also write about pollution
and other problems that worry people.

I do much of my research in libraries.
To find the most up-to-date information,
I visit special science libraries.
I talk to experts on the telephone,
or interview them in person.
Preparing to write the book *Elephant Woman:
Cynthia Moss Explores the World of Elephants*,
I talked with Cynthia Moss about her elephant
studies in Kenya, Africa.

Sometimes I travel to learn about a subject,
or to take photographs.

My work has taken me to deserts and mountains
and other wild places. It has also taken me
to dirty, smelly places. For my book
Throwing Things Away, about garbage
and other solid waste, I visited dumps and landfills.

By my desk are colorful tiles from Mexico.
They remind me of my trip to Mexico
with artist Bob Marstall.

His paintings illustrate my story
of a monarch butterfly that flies
to Mexico for the winter.
The book is called
*An Extraordinary Life: The Story
of a Monarch Butterfly.*

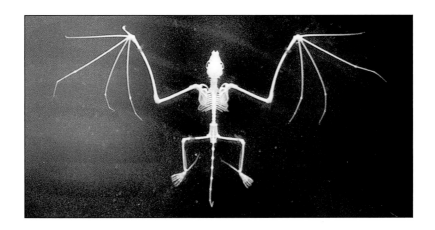

Animal bones and postcards from my travels decorate my office.

So do drawings from children I meet.

When I visit their schools, they often ask me
if I have a favorite book. I don't.

Each book is special and different from the others.
My fiction books are sparked by happenings
in my own family.

In 1983, I married Susan Klein, a teacher.
We live in West Nyack, New York
with our two children, Jesse and Rebecca.
The fun of roughhousing with them
and reading picture books to them
inspired me to write *Octopus Hug*.

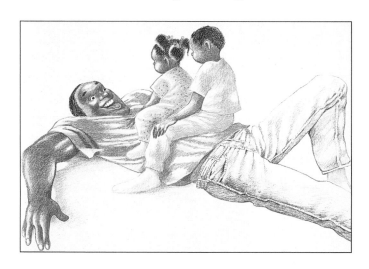

Now Jesse and Rebecca are too big for roughhousing, but Susan and I still read to them.

In 1994, when Jesse was in fourth grade, I took him with me to Florida. There we saw wild dolphins and I interviewed Randy Wells for my book *Dolphin Man: Exploring the World of Dolphins.*

I hope to take Rebecca on an adventure like this, too.

Writing happens anywhere, anytime.
On a walk one spring, I thought of ideas for this book.
All of my books and magazine articles
begin with a single piece of paper.
On it I jot down ideas. As I do research
I discover more ideas and events that I want to include.
Sometimes I make an outline of the flow of ideas.
Other times the outline develops
as I do more research and begin to write.
For many of my books, I first wrote a few sentences
on a lined yellow pad, then typed them on paper.
I repeated the process with some new sentences.
I read the typed words again and again.
I made many changes before typing
the final manuscript that I sent to a publisher.

Now I write sentences that appear on my computer screen.
I still read them again and again to find ways to make them clear and to make the subject fascinating.

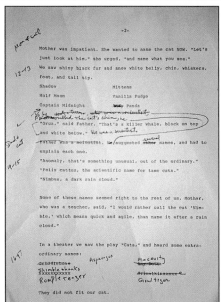

Even though I have written more than eighty books,
I am still learning how to be a better writer.

On school days I rise early to make lunches
for Jesse and Rebecca.

When everyone leaves for school,
the cats and I have the house to ourselves.

I don't write every day.
I may do research, write letters,
or talk to friends on the telephone.

I need a long stretch
of quiet time
in which to write.
Sometimes I take a nap,
then stay up very late writing.

Writing is sitting-down work, so I need to exercise.
Many days I walk three miles
to and from the post office for the mail.
I play volleyball and basketball.
I love to surf fish.

When I stand at the edge of the ocean —
so vast, wild, and mysterious —
I wonder what lies beneath its surface.
And I remember standing by the edge of a pond
when I was a boy and my curiosity about nature began.

Other Books by Laurence Pringle

Animal Monsters: The Truth about Scary Animals; Everybody Has a Bellybutton: Your Life Before You Were Born; Naming the Cat; Taking Care of the Earth: Kids in Action

About the Photographer

Tim Holmstrom is a freelance photographer. He lives in Connecticut. Tim became interested in photography when he was a teenager. He studied film and television in school. Tim travels a lot and uses four 35 millimeter cameras. He traveled to Asia to take pictures of the children there. He traveled to New York City to take pictures for Richard C. Owen Publishers' book *New York City Buildings*.

Acknowledgments

Photographs on pages 6, 7, 12 (top), 16, 17 (bottom), 24, 28 (bottom), courtesy of Laurence Pringle. Photograph on page 12 (bottom) by Jo McMillen. Photograph on page 18 by Christine Pratt. Photographs on page 20 by Laura Pakaln. Photograph on page 31 by Sean Pringle. Picture on page 10 from *Nature and Science* Vol. 3 No.18 / July 25, 1966 courtesy of Laurence Pringle. Illustration on page 11 and dinosaur poster on page 14 from *Dinosaurs! Strange and Wonderful*. Text copyright 1995 by Laurence Pringle. Illustrations copyright 1995 by Carol Heyer. Published by Boyds Mills Press. Reprinted with permission. Illustration on page 22 from *Octopus Hug*. Text copyright 1993 by Laurence Pringle. Illustrations copyright 1993 by Kate Salley Palmer. Published by Boyds Mills Press. Reprinted with permission.

Meet the Author titles

Verna Aardema *A Bookworm Who Hatched*
David A. Adler *My Writing Day*
George Ancona *Self Portrait*
Jim Arnosky *Whole Days Outdoor*
Frank Asch *One Man Show*
Joseph Bruchac *Seeing the Circle*
Eve Bunting *Once Upon a Time*
Lynne Cherry *Making a Difference in the World*
Lois Ehlert *Under My Nose*
Denise Fleming *Maker of Things*
Douglas Florian *See for Your Self*
Jean Fritz *Surprising Myself*
Paul Goble *Hau Kola Hello Friend*
Ruth Heller *Fine Lines*
Lee Bennett Hopkins *The Writing Bug*
James Howe *Playing With Words*
Johanna Hurwitz *A Dream Come True*
Eric A. Kimmel *Tuning Up*
Karla Kuskin *Thoughts, Pictures, and Words*
Thomas Locker *The Man Who Paints Nature*
Jonathan London *Tell Me a Story*
George Ella Lyon *A Wordful Child*
Margaret Mahy *My Mysterious World*
Rafe Martin *A Storyteller's Story*
Patricia McKissack *Can You Imagine*
Laura Numeroff *If You Give an Author a Pencil*
Jerry Pallotta *Read a Zillion Books*
Patricia Polacco *Firetalking*
Laurence Pringle *Nature! Wild and Wonderful*
Cynthia Rylant *Best Wishes*
Seymour Simon *From Paper Airplanes to Outer Space*
Mike Thaler *Imagination*
Jean Van Leeuwen *Growing Ideas*
Janet Wong *Before it Wriggles Away*
Jane Yolen *A Letter from Phoenix Farm*

For more information about the Meet the Author books
visit our website at www.RCOwen.com or call 1-800-336-5588